Story texts based on scripts written by Samantha Hill, Bridget Hurst and Dave Ingham

Illustrations from the TV animation produced by Tiger Aspect

PUFFIN BOOKS
Published by the Penguin Group: London, New York, Australia, Canada,
India, Ireland, New Zealand and South Africa
Penguin Books Ltd, Registered Offices: 80 Strand, London WC2R 0RL, England

puffinbooks.com

First published 2010

Made and printed in Italy

ISBN: 978-0-141-33162-1

characters created by

lauren child

My favourite and BEST Charlie and Lola ANNUAL 2011

This ANNUAL belongs to:

PUFFIN

Contents

I have this little sister Lola.
She is small and very funny.
Lola loves finding out about **new** things.

"Oh yes, Charlie, I want to KNOW
everything about **everything**!"

Our ABSOLUTELY best and most FAVOURITE places

Charlie and Lola love going to the **seaside** and to Grandma and Grandpa's **house**.

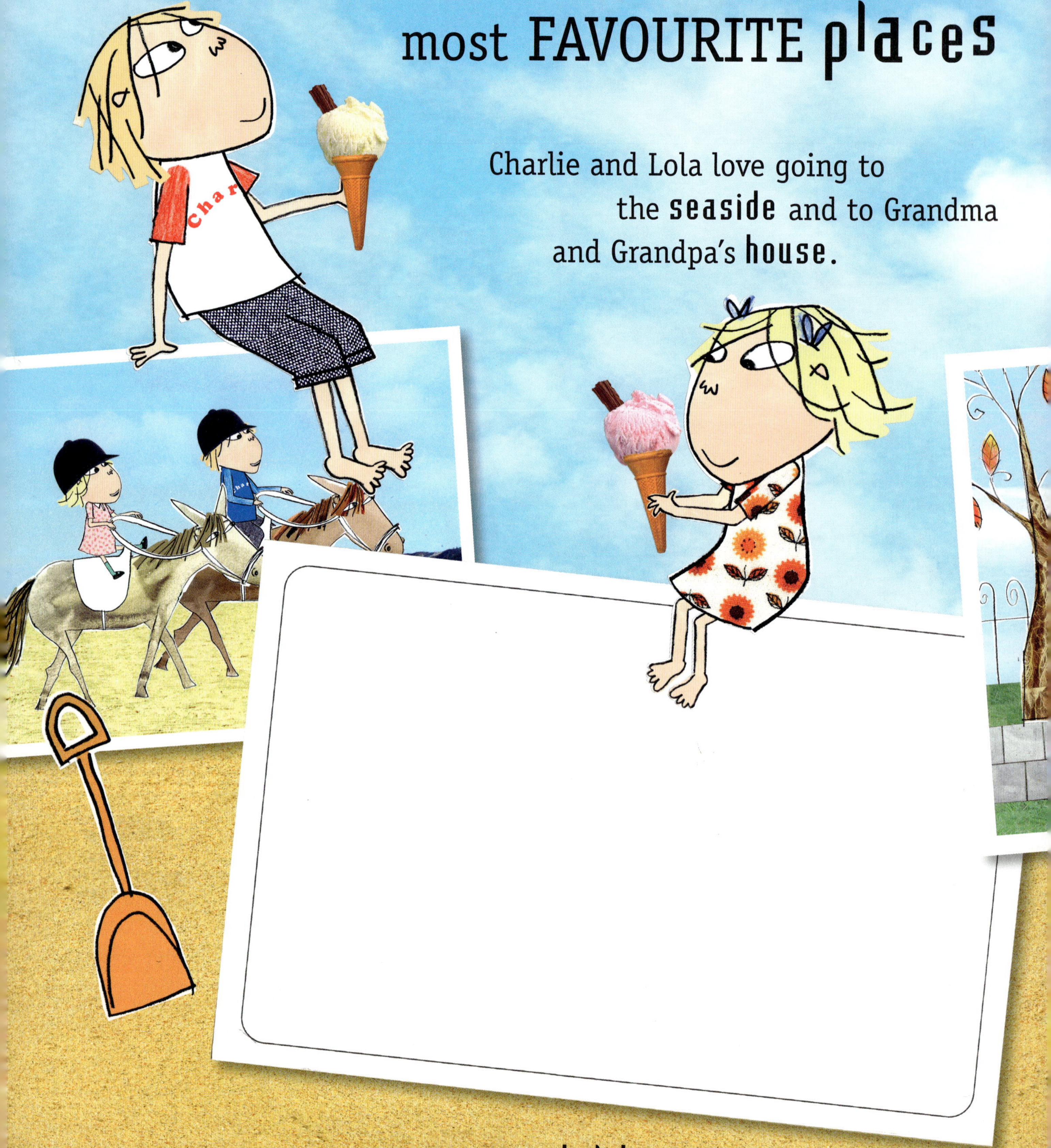

Where would you like to go on **holiday**? To the beach, a forest or a fairy-tale castle? Draw a picture here.

Where is your **best** and most **favourite** place? Draw a picture of yourself there.

My most **favourite** place is:

. . . .

My **completely** FAVOURITE way to get there is:

. . . .

Lotta and Marv like going to the **park** with Charlie and Lola too.

My **absolutely** best thing to do in my favourite place is:

. . . .

. . . .

I am inventing an INVENTION

I have this little sister Lola.
She is small and very funny.

Lola says, "Charlie, what are you reading?"

I say, "A book about **inventions**. Me and Marv need to **invent** something for a school project."

Lola asks, "What is an **invention**?"

So I say,
"An **invention** is something NEW that helps people do things better or faster or easier."

And Marv says,
"Like the **telephone**."

"But we already have a **telephone**," says Lola.

So I say,
"I know. But a very long time ago, people didn't have telephones."

Then Lola asks,
"But if there were no telephones, how could I tell Lotta about my new drawing?"

And I say,
"You would have to walk to her house."

"But it's a very, very, VERY long way to Lotta's house," says Lola.

"I would have to
get Mum to take me in the car."

So I say,
"But Lola, a very long time ago,
cars weren't invented, either.
You'd have to go by horse."

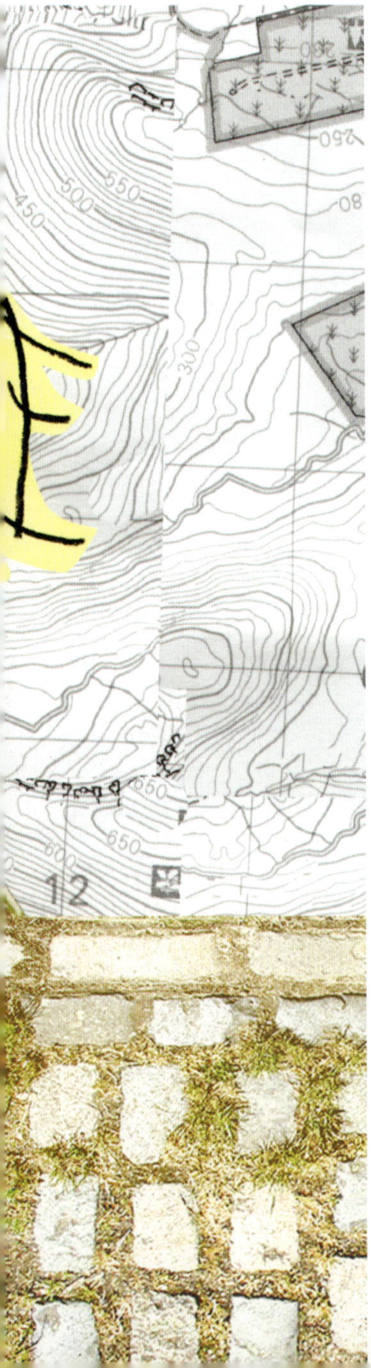

"Oh!" says Lola.

Lola says,
"Cars and telephones are very good inventions.
I'm going to make an invention all on my OWN."

So I say,
"Lola, it's not easy to invent something
that is very, VERY clever."

But Lola says,
"I can! I can invent
something.
You'll see!"

"Marv," I say,
"we must think of a useful **invention**."

And Marv says, "I've got it!
How about a **machine** that can walk Sizzles
when it's rainy outside."

Lola points at our drawing.
"But Sizzles's paws will never reach the pedals," she says.
"His legs are tiny!"

And I say,
"Oh! You're right."

"Well," says Marv,
"it would have been a good **invention**."

Then I say,
"We'd better come
up with something else."

Then Lola says, "Look, Charlie.
I am an actual inventor.
I invented a two-coloured crayon.
It's for when you want to draw
using green and blue."

"But what if you want to use red?"
asks Marv.

And Lola says, "Well...
I've got loads more inventions!"

"We need a good idea,
and quickly," I say.

"Hmmm," says Marv.
"It is quite tricky.
All the good inventions have been done."

Then I say, "I've got it!
We can make an AMAZING apple picker-upper!
It will pick up all the apples
that have fallen from the trees."

So Marv says,
"What would it look like?"

I say,
"It's made out of two bicycles
that are attached to a **vacuum** cleaner.
If we pedal really, really fast,
all the **apples** will get sucked up
and then tossed into the wheelbarrow."

So I ask Mum if we can use
the vacuum cleaner.

But she says no.

"Oh no!" says Marv.
"That was our BEST idea.
Now what?"

Later, Lola says,

"Have you thought of lots of clever and useful inventions?"

"We haven't got any," I say.

"Oh dear!" says Lola. "Maybe you are NOT inventors."

"But we have to be!" I say. "Our project is due tomorrow."

"What are we going to do?" asks Marv.

So we start thinking, and Lola starts picking up some of our mess...

Soon Lola gets stuck
to everything
with sticky tape...

...but then Lola has an idea...

"Look at me, Charlie!" says Lola.
"I'm all covered in mess."

So I say, "Yes. Thanks for cleaning up, Lola."

But Lola says,
"No, Charlie. Look at me. I'm an inventor. See?
All the things are on me.

There's a spot for
pencils
and
crayons
and
clips.

Now everything
is all tidy."

Marv says, "Lola, that is brilliant!
Can we borrow it for our project?"

"But will people think it is
really, REALLY useful?" asks Lola.

And Marv says, "Yes! Yes! They will!"
"And we do too!" I say.

So Lola says,
"I really completely am an inventor!"

Then Marv says,
"What should we call your invention?"

And Lola says,
"The very clever-ish and extremely useful-ish messy dress tidy-upper!"

AMAZING and very interesting inventing FACTS

Did you know that the first **rocket** was launched into actual **space** 60 years ago? It was used to send a **satellite** very high into the sky.

Marbles are made of **glass** now but the first ever marbles were made out of **clay**. The Romans used to play **games** with them.

The first proper **aeroplane** was built by tw brothers called Orville and Wilbur Wright. They flew it in 1903, before Grandpa was even a baby.

Can you think of some other very useful **inventions**? It could be something you use every day or something very strange and **special**.

The best **invention** I have ever seen is:

I would really like to **invent**:

"Hello, Lotta!"

How to make an ever-so-CLEVER telephone invention

You will need:

Two paper cups
A pencil
Two paper clips
A very long piece of string
(1–2 metres long)

1. First use your pencil to poke a small **hole** in the bottom of both cups. Ask a grown-up to help.

2. Push one end of the **string** through the outside of the first cup.

3. Tie this end to a **paper clip**. The **paper clip** will stop the **string** from falling out of the cup.

4 Take the other long end of the **string** and push it through the second cup. Tie this end to a **paper clip**. Your cups should now be connected by a long piece of **string**.

5 You can **decorate** your new phone with crayons, glitter and coloured paper!

Your extremely special **telephone** is ready to be used. All you need to do is hold one end and ask a **friend** to hold the other. Make sure the **string** is very straight and tight. Now you can take turns to **speak** into the cup and hold it to your ear to **listen**!

I'm just NOT keen on spiders

I have this little sister Lola.
She is small and very funny.

Lola isn't keen on spiders. She says,
"They're always dangling and running about."

Lola says,
"Spiders are BIG
and they are hairy."

I say, "But Lola, none
of them, NOT one, is
as BIG and hairy
as you! Just think
how BIG and hairy
YOU would
look to a spider."

Then I say,
"Do you remember
there was a time when
you didn't like beetles?"

Use these stickers for **how to make an ever-so-clever telephone invention** on pages 28–29

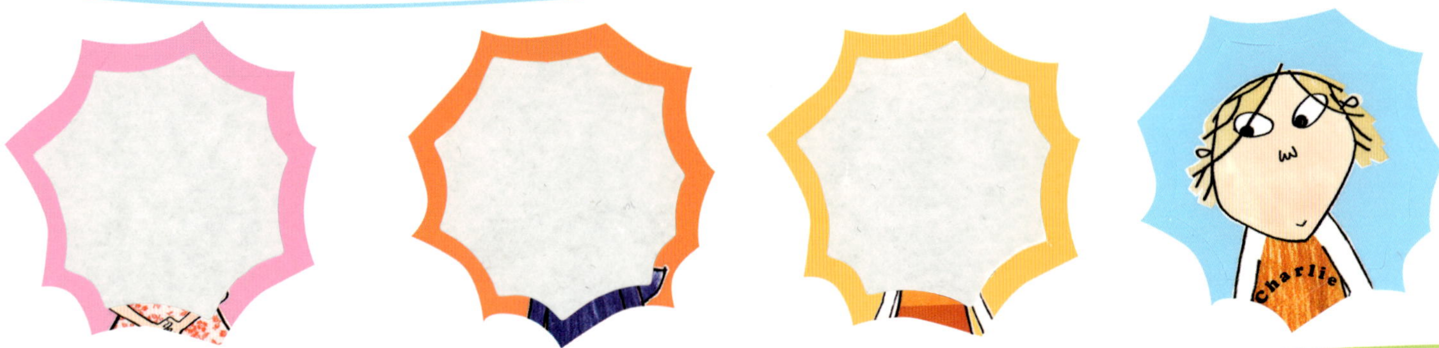

Use these stickers for **a very webby maze game** on pages 38–39

Use these stickers to **make a completely interesting bug jar** on pages 40–41

Then I tell her,

"Spiders are really clever.

They can walk upside down!"

And Lola says,

"That IS clever, Charlie."

"Beetles are funny, Charlie,"

says Lola.

"They get stuck on their backs

and wiggle their

funny little

legs!

So you see, I'm really

just NOT keen on spiders."

Use these stickers for **i spy with my very good eyes** on pages 58–59

Charlie and Lola™

Here are some extra stickers just for fun!

Then Lola says, "But I don't like those webby things."

So I say, "If you look closely, spiderwebs are really AMAZING. They come in ALL kinds of patterns and are really STRONG."

"Yes, Charlie," says Lola. "They really are completely very AMAZING, aren't they!"

Then I ask,
"Shall we put him **outside** now?"

"Oh no, not NOW, Charlie,"
says Lola.
"I've made a house for our spider and we're going
to have a spider tea party!"

A very webby MAZE game

Spider is having a very special spidery TEA party and the first player to join him in his web is the WINNER!

Use your favourite colouring pencils and crayons to decorate your game. You can make some counters using the stickers in the middle of this book – just stick them on to some card and cut them out (you could ask a grown-up to help). You will need dice to play this game.

How to play:

Choose a counter and put it down on the start square. Each player rolls the dice and moves their counter the number of spaces shown. If you land on a square with a forfeit you have to do exactly what it tells you – no cheating! Whoever reaches Spider first is the WINNER.

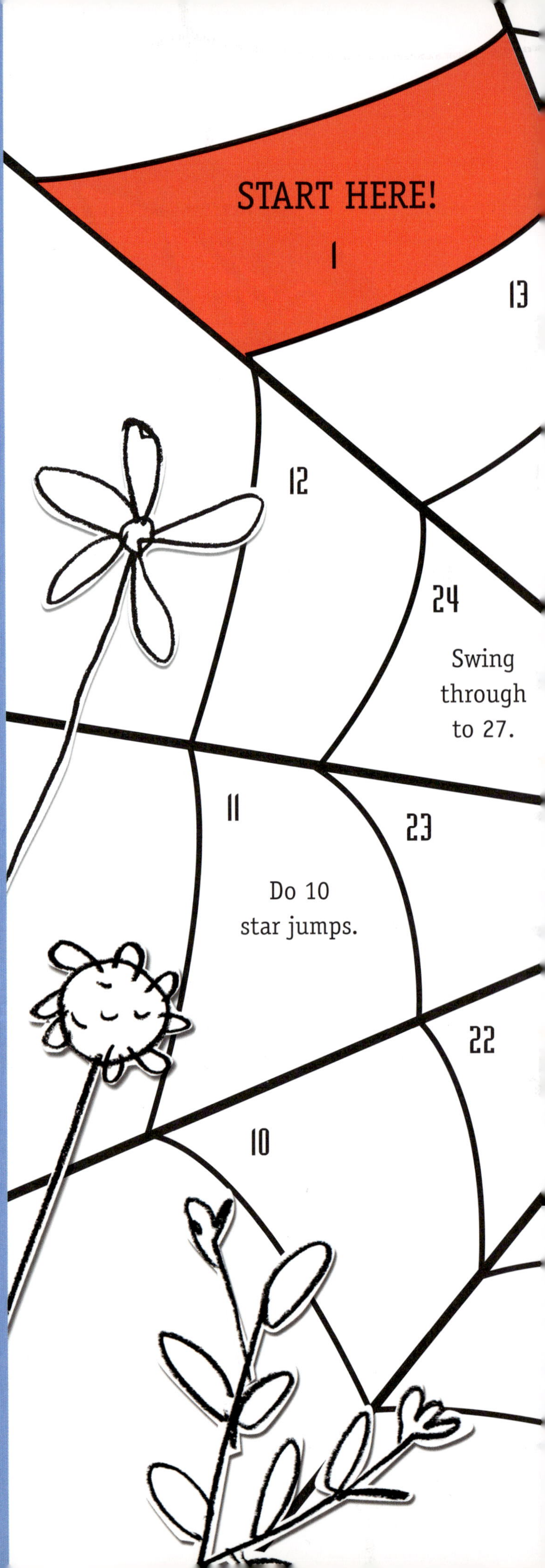

2
3
4
14
15
You're stuck in the web!
Miss a go.
5
26
27
28
16
5
Oops! Spider's left a
hole here. Go back
3 spaces.
Unlucky!
Back to
the start!
29
17
THE END!
You've won!
6
18
Do 10 hops on
your left leg.
21
20
19
7
Scuttle forward
4 spaces.
9
8

Make a COMPLETELY interesting bug jar

You will need:

An old plastic or glass jar (make sure you peel off the label and wash it before you use it)

A grown-up to help you punch some air holes in the jar lid

A long loop of string

Sticky tape

Some leaves or grass to make the bugs feel at home

1 Take your jar and ask a grown-up to help you punch some air holes in the jar lid. This will help your bug to breathe properly.

2 Put some leaves or grass inside your jar, leaving enough room for you to see the bugs clearly.

3 Make a carry strap for your jar by looping your string around the base and sticking it to the sides.

Make your own especially INTERESTING **bug jar** and watch all your most **favourite** insects. See how they **play**, what **noises** they make and even how they **sleep**!

4 You can decorate your bug jar with stickers from this book, or even some glitter.

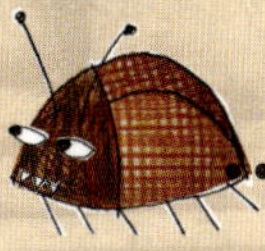

5 Now you're ready to use your bug jar. Try catching some in your jar and drawing them.

REMEMBER – only keep insects in your special **jar** for an hour or two and always put them back where you FOUND them!

Charlie's CREEPY-crawly FACTS

Charlie knows some extremely very good **facts** about CREEPY and very **crawly** bugs.

The world's LARGEST **spider** lives in South America. It is so heavy it can't live in a **web**, and has to live in a **burrow** instead.

Did you know that **ants** can carry more than THREE times their **weight**?

Ladybirds are very useful to gardeners because they **eat** all the tiny **pests** like greenfly.

Here are some EXTREMELY good **creepy-crawly** jokes

Why was the beetle forced to leave the **park**?

Because he was a **litter-bug**!

Why do bees **hum**?

Because they don't know the **words**!

What is an insect's favourite **game**?

Cricket!

What do you call a **greedy** ant?

An **anteater**!

Do you know any **funny** jokes too?

I really ABSOLUTELY must have glasses

I have this little sister Lola.
She is small and very funny.
Lola is thinking about seeing
because tomorrow Mum is taking her
to the optician to have her eyes tested.

Lola says,
"But my eyes do not need testing, Charlie."

So I say,
"But going to the optician is fun.
You get to find hidden pictures
in lots and lots of
coloured dots."

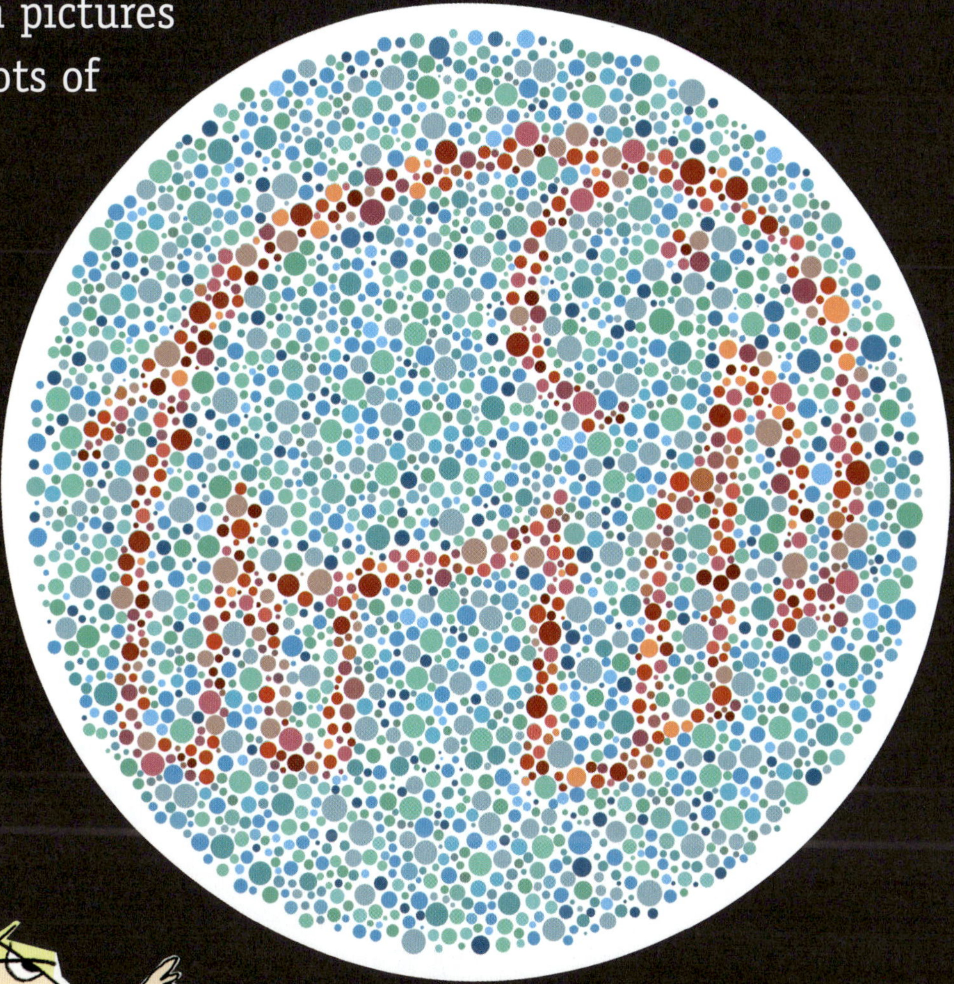

And Lola says,
"Dots, Charlie?
I love dots!"

Lola says,
"I can actually see very well.
I can see my spaghetti, and my bowl,
and my spoon, and my pink milk.
AND I can see YOU!

So I really absolutely do not need
to have an eye test."

At school,
Lola says, "Look! Mini's got glasses!"

And Lotta says,
"Where did you get your glasses, Mini?"

"They are especially very nice and flowery!"
says Lola.

And Mini says,
"I went to the optician. She said that I need glasses because everything I see is slightly fuzzy."

Later on, Lola says,
"Charlie, I can't wait
to go to
the eye tester!
I am going to get
some flowery glasses."

So I say, "Lola,
you'll only get glasses
if you really,
really need them."

And Lola says,
"But I DO
really need them...

...because I
cannot see that
pink biscuit...

...and I cannot
see my yellow
toothbrush...

... and now I can
definitely not see at all."

So I say,
"That's because it is dark."

And Lola says,
"Oh, yes! But when I get
my new glasses,
I'll be able to see
in the dark."

I say,
"No you won't, Lola."

But Lola says,
"I will, Charlie!
I will!"

The next day,
Lola says,
"Can I try on your glasses, Mini?"

But Mini says,
"The optician told
me it's not a good idea
because everyone's
eyes are different.
My glasses might make
your eyes a bit achy."

So Lola says,
"But how will I know which
glasses will look nice on me?"

Mini says,
"Oh, that's easy. At the optician's,
you try on lots of glasses
to see what you like best!"

And Lola says,
"I can't wait!
I can't wait!"

After school,
Lola and I go to
the optician's.

Lola looks at all
the different glasses.

When it's her turn
to see the optician,
Lola says,
"See you later, Charlie...
with my glasses!"

On the way home, Lola says,
"The optician said I absolutely do not need glasses, Charlie."

So I say,
"That's good! It means your eyes are very strong."

And Lola says,
"But I really, really wanted glasses."

Then I say,
"I have an idea!"

Lola and I cut and colour some pieces of paper.

We sprinkle glitter, stick on sparkly stars and add squiggly lines until we make...
an absolutely most PERFECT pair of glasses.

At school, Lola wears her new glasses.
Lotta has made some too!
Mini says, "I like your glasses, Lola."
And Lola says, "Yes, glasses can be fun even
if you don't need them!"

Some extremely most PERFECT glasses

Lola loves her COMPLETELY special glasses. You can make your very OWN pair too. All you need to do is trace the glasses on the next page and use them as a template. You can colour them in and maybe add some sparkly glitter, pretty paper or even some stickers to make them COMPLETELY perfect.

Trace the templates on to
some thick **paper** or **card**,
cut them out and **glue** the arms in place.
Your glasses are ready to **decorate**!

I spy with my VERY good eyes

Can you see all the animals in this EXTREMELY green and leafy jungle? Add Charlie and Lola too.

Lola says, "I have found out so many completely very interesting things today!"

And I say, "What else would you like to find out about, Lola?"

And Lola says, "Oh, I don't need to find out any more, Charlie. I think I know completely, absolutely EVERYTHING now!"